MOTHERBOARD

Attention schools and businesses: For discounted copies and
large orders please contact the publisher directly.

Kallisto Gaia Press Inc.
1801 E. 51st Street
Suite 365-246
Austin TX 78723
(254) 654-7205
www.kallistogaiapress.org

Cover Photo: Renee Rossi
Edited by: Tony Burnett

ISBN: 978-1-952224-11-9

MOTHERBOARD

poems

Renee Rossi

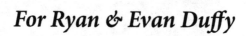

For Ryan & Evan Duffy

Table of Contents

SOMETIMES, A WOMAN STANDS UP

Sometimes a man stands up during supper
and walks outdoors, and keeps on walking.
                                                            - Rilke

Her arms must be pale. Mid-supper, a woman
removes a glass from the shelf and breaks it on the floor.

She takes off her apron, it may be a gown. No longer
a mother. Finger pads rubbed raw,

she puts on her coat and touches the door.
There might be a late autumn wind whipping outside,

thrashing what few dead leaves hold steadfast
to swaying limbs. For it is dark, and still

no stars. But she has waited long enough and can see stars
in daylight. She has given everything: blood, milk,

muscle, sinew, and bone. The lake laps at her feet,
wanting to take more of her shoreline. Maybe her toes

have never felt floorboard grain this way. She knows
of the six tastes, salt is the only one a human cannot live without.

And how it dissolves in a boiling pot, how it concentrates
in tears, how tears carry crystals of the mind's sorrow and fear.

There is an herb called *Ashoka* that *takes away a woman's sorrow,*
its red bark given to a woman after loss of a child, husband

or a dream. It helps bind that empty space in the womb, that wide
open space in a Rousseau painting where a young maiden touches

a green leaf, thinks of a lover and the silent kingdom, and a
lioness
stares back at her. What she's never held, she does not know
how to let go of.

And there may be a temple somewhere with a priestess
swinging a censer,
the smoke coasting along the flight path of swallows. It reaches
her.

UNDERWATER BEES

That was before the seed
cracked open,
before the water broke,
before grackles lined up
on stoplight wires,

when minnows swarmed
like underwater bees,

before you and I were born,
or imagined embryos from
thousands of immature eggs
lodged inside us,
before we knew the eighteen ways
to make a baby.

Hollow balls of cells.
Everything a woman will ever have,

there at birth, and dwindling
like hairs that wrap themselves
into nests in the drain.
And fried eggs, eggs over easy,
and egg whites. Prom dresses
with taffeta linings, the white silk
christening outfit, and baby toes.

And planning. And devising.
There must be
harmless ways to feed an idea.

SELF-PORTRAIT OF A BIRTH FROM HAND-HELD MIRROR

The last time you will ever be judged as a fruit,
      cervix ripe as a pomegranate,
bursting fine conjunctival vessels,
petechial hemorrhages budding the afterbirth
of sutures through a torn perineum, the crowning
      moment, a child

      trailing umbilical cord a right and wrong way,
the absolute mocking him from
a Where's Waldo roadmap into the future.
Little dabs of silver nitrate swabbed over his eyes.
It will be nothing to love him so much
      you can't give answers when he later sees

a missed abortion in your medical book, the bones
of a fetal skeleton entombed in a mother's womb.
      Why do they call it a seed, he'll ask,
when seeds grow into plants. Why are there maggots

under the compost lid, the same ones that crawl
      on an amputee's stump
after you've unwrapped the dirty bandage

but you won't tell him this or why the neighbor asks
      you to bury the dead hummingbird
that's thrown its body against her picture window
because you're used to death,

you've cross-clamped arteries and veins
leading in and out of that place
that connects the two of you.

Your little prayer book of childhood opens
      to the Acts of Contrition. Where a fetal heart beats
in a jar of formaldehyde. You touch his soft fontanelle.

Our Fathers Took Lithium

Outside, where I've buried three mice,
snow sticks to birch branches.

Spring, you say, makes us all runny
and water inside our blood expands

though I know it runs undiluted in our veins.

This jay smacks at a window
trying to eat cluster flies inside.

Our fathers had the spring madness.
Cold nights, sap gathered in their roots

and days, earth surged up their veins—
this, our shared history. You teach

my tender hands to tap maple trees,
splice sap lines, run tubes through the woods

unlike my father who penned Post-it
notes, his yellow fetters of madness

stuck all over the house.
Our fathers took Lithium.

Come spring, let us dance with sparrows

for seeds in the thawing lilac bush
as water trickles off the roof,

carrying raucous particles of
angst and mineral and madness.

SPRING'S WRATHFUL DEITIES

When Persephone disappeared, Demeter
did not eat or drink for nine days.
For my mother, who left too early,
I gathered and inscribed
eggs with wrathful deities.
But, I have no daughters.

~

Eutori is a life space, a place
to contemplate the living or
stand back and watch results
of wind. Spring, mud season, is here

though a late snow tears gold
from our ears. A myth says
there was a blood sea
at the beginning of the world.

Colt's foot blooms in ditches,
bright yellow temple hairs
amidst green blankets of hope.
A sparrow pecks at the feeder,
late snow frosts fiddlehead ferns.

~

Stratus clouds, they're the only ones
joining us as street level.

~

Shantideva says an uncompassionate act
is like planting a dead tree.

The loss of daughter to mother,
and mother to daughter,
is the essential female tragedy.

On cloudy nights, dung beetles
have difficulty orienting themselves.
They need sun.

TOWER OF MOTHERS

after the bronze sculpture by Kathë Kollwitz

In Japanese, *komorebi* means dappled
sunlight through trees, something
         untranslatable,
like the scent of sun
in your child's hair,

or the bronze Tower of Mothers
who face outward, breasts and eyes
to the crowd, trying to shield their sons
         from going to war. Such angels

exist in a memory palace
where you put things in each room
         you want to memorize:

your 60s mother wrapped in the spiral
cord of a wall telephone, or
a witness tree planted near a cliff,
         an old picture of your son

holding a lemon the size of his head
next to a limoncello stand
in Naples. Not far from Pompei's
ruins where he marveled at penises
inscribed in stone as arrows to guide
illiterate to whorehouses.
         And how it all fell,

human bodies entombed in ash,
         beckoning, as laundry
dried on racks hung
from window casements.

But, you'll never forget all humans
come in to the world through
the gateway of a woman's body.

This practice of being a mother,
it's a type of dismemberment.

PETALS

Spread out on the floor, *Die*
Geschichte, the history,
and a language primer, three-by-five cards,
vergessen, to forget, exhaling
each guttural syllable she works
past midnight on the college degree.
      Sleepless, I
wander in, robe clasped. *Sit*
down, come quiz me. Smoke curls
around words she already knows:
verboten, to forbid,
bedienen, to serve,
entschuldigen, to pardon.
      I am no longer
a child whose presence cuts short

her college prospects. 1974. The dishwasher
hums and thuds as it releases

∫

dry soap. Humming and thudding, the washer
careens off balance into a laundry wall.
      I cut up
her last strands of hair to hand-sew
into little pillows rimmed with lace.
No open casket or stiff-veins,
fingers plumped with latex, she waits
for us in a ten-pound-box
of bone and ash. No one
anymore. I glue her photos to a board
for the non-viewing service. A blond-
braided girl in the middle of a field,
eyes uplifted, long before

she's lost patience with this world,
her lips pursed in determination.

∫

Pursed in determination, her lips shape
smoke rings larger than Saturn's, fingers
caressing a cigarette as if it were

the joystick to another life. Molding
the ash tip to a fine point, she reads
about the Ming Dynasty and its curious custom
of foot binding. How the lotus petal feet
couldn't venture far from home—crimped,
cracked, and stinking foot
bones covered in delicate doll's
shoes. She drops a couple quarters

in my palm. *Run down to the corner*
and grab me some Kent Longs.

∫

Run down to the pharmacy
and pick me up
some Valium. She can sleep in
her wasted body or watch chickadees
pick suet off the crabapple. The commode sits
a foot away, obstinate. The hardest part,
she says, is the mind still being
so active. Not obstructed
bowels, outpatient chemo, or the stairs
she can no longer climb for the box
of quilting fabrics. While she dozes, she sees
the wedding ring quilt in a fitful dream.

Evening settles for a log-cabin
pattern in muted oranges.

∫

A log cabin quilt is draped
over her lap. Is it pyelo
or thrombophlebitis this time?
She writes in my baby book:
She went to school the first day
of kindergarten all by herself.
I wore a pleated skirt, white knee-socks.
She looks out the window of Jennings

onto Jefferson pretending to plant
a kiss goodbye on my forehead.

∫

A breathless kiss glances
my forehead, I am
in the cabin she designed
on this land she camped for years.
She calls to ask if the view of the lake's blocked
by white pines. Green-throated
warblers and spring peepers croon.
I hold the phone out over the deck:
Can you hear them? Trillium
bloom on the roadsides. I take
pictures of what we both pretend
she'll see. I must

∫

be climbing down the bungalow
stairs from under the sloping
eaves. Spread out on the floor
in front of her, columns
of German verbs: *I just don't get it,*
they put ge in front of everything.

A little hair pillow hangs
from my bed post with this Easter photo
from '65. Her powder-blue dress and ratted hair.
She's holding the fourth baby
in six years. I
                    monkey face
the camera while my younger brother holds
his already too-heavy head. My sister
with the wandering eye patched. My father
                    lost behind the shutter.
A young family collects in the red
Studebaker, heads for high Latin mass
in the crying room at St. Jude's,
patron saint of lost causes.

Under her breath, I hear her mutter
gestorben.

DAKINIS

The wild women have entered the woods—
they take their chances, they prance

on the forest floor. With leeches, they let
blood from cloudy souls passing through.

They throw their breasts over their shoulders
as they run. From house fires, clogged toilets,

laundry. It's known they tickle people to death
who wander too far into their realm

with quotidian troubles. The sun eats from
a porridge bowl in a Russian fairy tale, wanders

in, slips out. Who keeps time in these woods,
as they sleep on wood chips? The dancing,

fox trot and swirling dresses. No little
fabric-lined cubicles to dampen sound,

cities with fluorescent lights and fire lanes.
The ancients have a chapter in a book

that tells about the signs of dying,
the signs of a dead soul or those

living who can't reap the grain, spin
the wool, thread the needle, comb out

hemp. But they never mention wild women
and how, when you let them dance on your hut,

they bring you leaves that turn to gold.

My Father's Firearms

The cadets stand in a perfect line, uniformed,
one palm up, pistol on its side, barrel looking off

to the same place their eyes are pointed
in that old black-and-white photo of you

at the Police Academy inspecting their pistols.
Maybe you flipped cylinders to see if

bullets were placed correctly, touching smooth
shininess of barrel, letting the stock lay

unguarded in your palm to know in the way of a seer
what havoc this object might wreak in the future.

Maybe you were taking the pulse of the gun, to see
if it had a mind of its own. Or maybe, it was your way

of blessing a gun, inadvertently blessing those
young men whose faces had to learn dispassion

to be effective. They stand there looking off into
the future; serious, immobile, erect. I don't

pretend to know anything about guns, other than believing
they were the reason I couldn't sit in your lap as a child—

I asked you a hundred times if you'd ever shot anyone,
then fabricated stories that you'd race your squad car

onto burning streets, using judo kicks and karate chops
to wrest switchblades which would flip in the air and land

closed in your palm, the way the gun does in the picture,
almost meditatively as if your palm were a metal

magnet. They say you were an amazing shot.
The last time we drove around Belle Isle, it was winter.

You said, right there, right there, pointing to the spot
where you used to have target practice with the cadets.

How you had to watch for boats on the river.
It was a Detroit-heavy-sky day, and the water broke

in grey waves, but winter grasses swayed
to some heartbeat around the ponds and walkways

of Frederick Law Olmsted's sorriest jewel park—
still, you never answered me.

MOTHERBOARD

That we might walk into the woods with our kind, wearing dinosaur hats, lift a few stones and tufts of lichens, that we might find the rhizomic mat that connects us to one another.

My son used to eat sand in the sandbox when he was little. Many photos of him smiling, with sand around his lips and teeth. A little beach growing inside him, human sandpaper. We planted wildflowers and learned the difference between flame acanthus and passion vine. And he'd toddle out naked and snip wildflowers with his plastic scissors or fill my camera with photos he'd taken of the dog's eyes or anus up close. A whole roll of film spent photographing a pill bug rolling around after he lifted a stone and said: *there, I saved that one.* And I would let him do this of course, because I knew that one day in the future I'd regret it if I hadn't. We'd pretend we had a farm or a forest out back. He wanted to have a miniature pig in the yard. He would put his pants on backwards for preschool and I couldn't bear to ask him to change them around. Different colored socks. And he would call all kids *young Mikes.* Big trees and shafts of sunlight. For the little birds that would slam into our picture window in spring, we made pictures and signs telling them to turn around and go back into the woods. When the computer died, he took it apart and found the motherboard, glued baubles and gems on it, and gave it to me for Mother's Day.

WOMEN WHO LIE ALONE AT MIDNIGHT

Title from "Women in Labor" by Mary Ruefle

Women who lie alone at midnight
work daily in the fields of their longing.

They toil at resisting, tear
clothing off scarecrows,

melt blackbirds on electrical wires,
keep time with their slippers.

Debilitated planets, where are you?
These midnight women can't speak to you—

Mercury has flown off with their voices.
Nacre in the heart clogs memory.

A pearl is a pearl is a pearl in the underworld,
where flights of fancy dance on wooden feet.

Analysis of the Rose as Sentimental Despair

after Cy Twombly's 5 paintings of the same name

Say goodbye, Catullus,
to the shores of Asia
Minor said Cy,

painting blooms through the doorway
and something from Rilke
scratched in palimpsest
about standing on fishes.

The rose.
I saw it grow old
in little pieces.

**

The lost stars in Houston,
a sliver moon. Icy,
poor, beautiful stars.

City overpasses, the lack of
urban planning. An old live oak's

lost leaves and limbs
droop to the ground.
Scientists found black holes

collide, they've found gravitational
waves. It happened.
1.3 billion years ago

and Einstein was right—
our lives less than moments,
colliding, colluding, yours

no longer than mine.
Your black hair, stories
I work with the fear
of losing the memory of you.

Jonquils, crocuses, tulips
in February. What is
a lifespan? The center of

a rose as despair
or garments made of macaw
feathers and fibers by Andean
tribes from the BC?

You would have sat it out
on the museum sofa.

**

Driving seven-lane freeways
past large old churches, you understand
they've torn down your childhood home

by the railroad, stadium gone,
Brewster projects gone.

This city blooms,
a brown rose
on a scalpel's edge.

Ground doves dine above the din
as if it were a century ago,
or a century from now.

A woman builds fractals
out of starfish wired together and
hangs them from the museum ceiling—

inverted stars; call it hopeful,
this culling of animals.

Didn't we always want
so many *things*? We stole
gold from the Aztecs.

**

Didn't we always want
to do so many *things*?

Chemistry & biology & medicine &
heartbeats & primrose & hyacinth
bean vine. An ache
to learn everything,
but we planted a Japanese maple
in honor of our capacity
to forget it all.

**

The exhaustive pattern of skies
seen on road trips: cloud
after cloud painting on
Einstein's ceiling, concealing

black holes and space particles
orbiting in their own orbits,

one woman's collage of an egg
from bits of fabric. Only a woman
collages with linen and gauze,

the template of skin,
before she feels anonymous.
Before the sooty skies
and blown apart railroads

in Puntarenas, the empty
container ships in its gulf—
everything decays if left

on its own, even cement.
Perhaps that's what's left
at the center of a rose,

its impermanence.

THETA

A computer gave you your Greek name,
raped and beaten goddess, found
curbside struggling to breathe

as you were left, as you are, nameless,
violet tongue too swollen
to lick your own wounds.

You must have been cold a long time
not to feel your missing teeth,
the which-way-ever of your lips,

fingernails ripped from their beds, scarlet
lake, gentian, and rose madder down your body
to its bruised and dangling toes. You are

wired and stapled and stitched and
still not whole, not ever whole.
How a bruise in nature, it grows

to you, monstrous goddess Theta,
tubed and lined, and not feeling now,
not feeling fine. From the angles

of your body, cosine and sine, broken
arms jut out beyond
                your lacerated heart, refusing

to fold back over your chest, refusing
these coins I want to place
                upon your bluing eyes.

Θ

TODAY'S LIST OF DENIALS

The sparrows that nest in the laundry exhaust spit out their rejected young onto the cement below, filmy eyes bulging like flies, little beaks open with silent cries, as mother passes them over again and again to bring food to her healthy young.

The chief cardiac surgeon walks by our operating room several times each day during bypass to smoke while the fellows build new coronaries for the two-pack-a-day smoker lying on the table.

And you and I – we eat Chinese take-out with our bare hands as we talk about ruptured aortas and units of blood while the Bosnian ex-mine sweeper with three bullet holes in his belly fastens down our granite slab countertops, shiny verde moss.

BUDDHIST SLOGAN #21
Always maintain a joyful mind

Saturday morning at Monahan's,
a short-order restaurant
where hookers arrived
bleary eyed,
smoking cigarettes. They prefaced
everything with honey
because all their honey had dripped out.
Coins jingled
in their fur coat pockets.

I was fifteen and without
edges yet, only wanting
to make eggs sunny side up,
hash browns and warm coffee
with milk to melt
the hardness
in their leathery voices.

We'd look out plate glass
windows onto Jefferson
to our lapsed car capital
with its glint of
shiny metal and chrome
and swallow all
the grey skies had to offer—
a lone quarter on the formica table.

Cento from the Mummy Doctor

After Arthur Aufderheide

I have scores of eyes—

if someone wants to study them,
many of the penises resemble
vacated butterfly cocoons. I wash

my hands after touching a mummy
but, really, I'm just going through

the motions. I have never cared
to possess an entire mummy,
dissecting mummies is salvage

pathology. I'm waiting to find

someone who's really committed to eyes
before I give these away. I often think

about what these people were like,
what they did every day, how they took
care of their kids. Eyeballs are number one,

having the highest organ scores. I avoid

saying he's the oldest mummy. The moment
you say oldest, people will come

out of the woodwork and say
their mummy is a few years older.

DO WE KNOW HOW SHE SURVIVES?

No doubt one of her days is all the earth and all of infinity.
- Rilke

If you study earth too long
a coiled fiddlehead fern erupts
from a running stream,

rivulets of sweat on her forehead.
The blue jay takes no recess.
Later, beet greens emerge,

red-veined emeralds, leaf
edges sing a lullaby
to the wind. Eggshells

in compost, crushed empty
cages around vacant embryos.

How the cabbage rose opens
with the vulnerability of time
or a jet flare serrates sky.

You won't know why the cucumber
curls at the fence, why
the hungry line up at food banks,

how the cold winter
slakes the black raspberry
bush of its thorn

that punctures the skin just now
as Japanese beetles mate
mid-pole bean. Could this caesura

be a pine tree in morning mist
or the tractor's bush hog
creating freshly cut grass,

its scent the piercing cry of
her green-leaf volatiles?

FROM MOTOR CITY MULCH

If you take I-75 north from Toledo, you can smell Detroit's aroma—
rendered fat next to funeral pyres of slag and smokestacks
sprouting from Motor City mulch. When asked what suburb I come from,
I say Detroit where children play in oil slicks like little bruises
in the shadows. Where else could you live as a troll
along a Rouge River? The gift that place gave me in never having to grieve
leaving it. A place where I once stood waiting for a lift
after my car battery was stolen and pimps lined up for me. I learned to
water ski on the Detroit River and still am picking amoebas from my ear canals.
Something in the water there killed humans and alewives
our side of the Ambassador Bridge. My father, the lieutenant,
said bodies would float because of the gases (they were never Canadians:
riparian rights separated us from a country where they didn't hunt humans).
On clear nights, the Big Dipper ladled goodness over there,
and only badness on our side. On I-94, a huge billboard loomed
with the Marlboro man trying to ride his horse out of Detroit.
That's when I knew the auto industry was in for it, though
my old boyfriend played Russian roulette badly, racing onto Woodward
in his Ford Fairlane past 8 Mile where the drunks routinely rammed
cars into phone poles. In our closet at home hid the '67 riots gear,
helmet, and billy club we were never supposed to touch. Switch-blades
my father confiscated: we devised stories about children who flipped them
open in the air, catching them closed without a nick.
My old house is officially in the ghetto now and this reminds me of

the Buddha who says we are all part of the present and the past.
I know
I carry the ghetto in me. The Henry Ford Museum got Lincoln's chair,
the one Booth shot him in, next to pieces of the first factory lines—
I always thought this was a coup for Detroit, where you sit down on the job,
you lose. Henry Ford was our man, though.
They named half of Detroit after him including the hospital
where I learned to put breathing tubes in the ones who didn't make it:
the ones still warm and pliable, the ones who jumped
off overpasses, those finished off by rival gangs: my teachers
said it was for practice. Outside the hospital, I saw
rats large enough to lift manhole covers.
We all have to come from somewhere.

Epigenetics

I would have to go way back to remember something
I never knew. A mother's mother beating her for the
premature child born blue. An immigrant's undoing.
Your narrow range of stories I knew by heart: snakes
around your tent at Fort Hood, the heat, stomping on
grapes with your father to make wine, a scissor-tailed
flycatcher on the railing. Everything down to the right
word for the crossword puzzle. Your beautiful brain.
The stars. And the word "neuter," what the SPCA
advises. The rest swallowed into darkness.

A Dash for the Timber

The Buddha says we make the world with our thoughts

Horses' flared nostrils and panicked eyes stare out at us,
whereas cowboy eyes are smudged over in oil.
Frederic Remington paints *A Dash for the Timber*
from his Fifth Avenue studio. Horses running
from a posse, painted by a man overlooking
street cars. What gallops against the chest wall?

The hot sun, this Groundhog Day of 02/02/2020,
a palindromic anomaly. Horses have a range of vision
almost a full circle, while humans see only a 150 degree
arc. Remington asked friends to send him chaps so he could
paint them realistically. But the eyes of his horses came
from Apache wars. Like the tornado that whipped through

this city where I raised kids, bought shoes at Target, where
the corner grocery once stood, and memories lived
in the pecan tree and Shumard oak, now gone.
Rubble everywhere, a warzone, as horses
flare their nostrils to extract more oxygen.
Like the world is on fire. At a museum
few people stand in front of paintings

as it's Super Bowl Sunday. The city grew
in its Texas thirst for expansion, one cement highway
after another. Sometimes, hoof prints of danger gather
near the low thrum of city traffic and barbecued animals
pay tolls for living. Two men sit at the hotel's bar stools
watching the game on TV, beers cupped in hand,
while the ice machine clatters and heaves.

Horses see predators and hear the wild war cries
as an arrow pierces a cowboy reincarnated and tackled
on a grass field today in front of millions. The heart is
a damned skeptic. We are what we think, though,
believing that heart back alive in a slumped over cowboy
as his horse dashes away, half an eye on everything.

Jesus and the Ozone Hole

My son says he's looking for cumulonimbus clouds. You should hear how he says that. He's happy to see clouds. He asks if the cotton ball in his ear could be one, asks about the ozone hole. I tell him a tarp should be up there in the sky to protect us from the sun. He's grinning ear-to-ear, ultraviolet, reeking of kid as he puts on his bicycle helmet. I'd like to slow down your aging, I say. He doesn't get relativity. I don't either but I want to buy it for him. Actually, I think I spell that out for him, tell him I'm sorry he's learning predicates in school. The sun scalds the back of my neck as he runs next door trying to convert the neighbor's kid to Christianity. Even now as I wear my 45 sunscreen. Jesus is my homey, he laughs out through the holes in his bicycle helmet. I never taught him any of this. Swear on it, I say to the kid's mother. It's that ozone hole growing larger, leaking soap operas into these kids' heads. My son begs me to repeat the story of the boy who plugged a toilet with a Jesus Action Figure right before church. The house flooded. Too much Jesus, he says, shaking his nubby head.

IRRESPONSIBILITY IN EVERYTHING
Title line after Marina Tsvetaeva

Songbirds: we walk into woods early spring to find them. He knows where ice melts in marshes, where woodcocks take advantage of unshaded southern edges of forest. Where worms come to the surface in patches of melted snow, where mourning warblers hide within vegetation.

Mourning what? Childhood's lost habitats?

He sends me photos of the boreal owl which can find mice under snow by sonar. It's the asymmetrically placed ears fashioned strangely on its scalp. I imagine its skull. I imagine its waiting. I imagine my brother waiting patiently to take its photo. He also is excited by the ruffled grouse drumming on a downed log. Time passes slowly in that world.

When he was young, he won a bird-naming contest when other kids threw stones at cars.
The other kids also threw rotten eggs at cars on Devil's night.

Mephistopheles may have Faust's soul if he is ever content:
"I am part of the part that once was everything, part of the darkness which gave birth to light." Or simply that shadow part of the whole. The shadow of a Merlin falcon waiting for the right songbird.

There were songbirds on the calendars in the nursing home where my grandmother stayed at the end. Silent songbirds. When she died, I placed a ceramic cat on her body bag as she was fond of cats. When she was wheeled out on a gurney, people paid respects by bowing. Ceramic cats and pictures of songbirds on calendars. Somehow, that combination made it right.

Gone, the three ancient ladies who creaked on the greenhouse ladders (Roethke).

~

How is relationship the sharing of one's solitude with another?

I have spent an inordinate amount of time reading about chakras to find my weak chakra is *Manipura*, which means "lustrous gem" because it shines like the sun. Radiant glowing center. Its symbol, a lotus with ten petals. Within it is a downward pointing triangle surround by three T-shaped *svastikas*. Which were ultimately recast and refurbished into swastikas. And loss of power to manipulate our surroundings.

Ten fingers, ten petals, ten toes, the beginning of a new cycle, logarithms, decimals.
A fly in amber, forever.
A fly in ambush, frozen.
A fly flying ambivalently, forgotten.
A green bottle fly, amputated by an Orkin representative.

On the radio I hear that twenty percent of women have no sexual drive:
> -with/without ovaries or uteruses.
> -this is an untapped market, the investors reported.
> -there are new gadgets and pills being invented.

The goddesses can no longer hide in thickets as here, in an excerpt from the Druids:
> Drink from a well before sunrise.
> Wash in the morning dew, and adorn yourselves with
> > greenery....
> watch the sun come up,
> dance round the Maypole,
> and otherwise abandon yourself to the season.
> A woodland frolic culminating in indiscretion is the
> > order of the day.

~

There are more angels than wounds on this earth. I paraphrase a nun with a wimple from my Catholic grade school. Or maybe she said: Every life has a moment like this, one that breaks you into brand new pieces. Or maybe, she just scolded me for spitting out a piece of chewing gum into the air at the end of recess and having it land in my hair.

In my first youth, I would ask the nuns for a field trip to their convent.
In my second youth, I was not the woman my husband married. The truth about intimate relationships is they can never be better than the ones we have with ourselves.

There's epigenetics and memory and craving.
But the important thing to remember is that ultimately there are no tragedies.
Pir Vilayat Inayat Khan says: "Overcome any bitterness that may have come because you were not up to the magnitude of the pain that was entrusted to you. Like the mother of the world who carries the pain of the world in her heart."
Each of us is part of her heart.
Each of us carries a certain measure of cosmic pain.

I have witnessed more deaths than births. Deaths>>>>births*
The multiple universe idea
severely limits my hopes
to understand the world
or people who shoot turtles for fun.

*this is not reflective of society as a whole. It is a byproduct of being a doctor for thirty years and the fact there are only two ways to go in a hospital stairwell.

~

There was a Japanese man who loved his missing wife very much.
She was lost in the tsunami:
First he searched on land,
and along the beaches of Onogawa,
and in the forests and mountains,
and then he turned to the sea.
He could die of hypothermia,
entanglement, the bends....

The water wasn't clear. He called the oceans' sound *chirichiri*, the sound of hair burning or a snake hissing.

Another woman lost her daughter in the tsunami and prepared meals each day packed with pork soup, Salisbury steak, and deep-fried shrimp in special boxes that decomposed, and dropped them in the sea. Lunchbox prayers.

With an axe to break the frozen sea within us.
Aghora can be interpreted as "deeper than deep."
Sometimes, people fall through ice in ponds
and there is a space below, with no water.
And they live.
Even now, as the world's fresh water contracts.

~

The boys in the basement are at work again.
The stairs are like Jacob's ladder where he fought the angels and won.

Out my windows I see the tops of trees, the pink buds
at the tip of the crepe myrtle, the red oak, and the little leaf elm
peeking over the edge of the house. Something about trees
has always made me want to dance.

In my last life, I drowned in a deep ocean,
the philosophical Jyotisch astrologer told me

on my first reading. That is why I am
sometimes afraid of ocean. I watch
for tide change, wind change,
strong southern winds,
latitude lines, wear
an emerald on my pinkie finger

and claim *irresponsibility in everything,
except play.*

TANGERINES

After the snow settles, the new father has an exotic job
growing tangerines in a valley where you see snow-

capped mountains but the climate is temperate
and the mother is never sick and paints clouds, the mother

who wants to find a new world in her own personal snow globe,
but her father enrolls her in secretarial school,

so she leaves home to have a baby. We're all inside that
snow globe: father, mother, swinging crib, house

with pine tree and unattached garage. And memory, of which
there is none until preschool when you fall off a piano bench

and hit your head and the world grows sparkly and crystalline.
Or at age four when Kennedy's death plays over and over on TV

and all the ladies cry. And wear those hats. Your mother
never wore one of those hats. You were born under a dark moon

so inside the glass globe it's dark memories appearing
first. Snow globes came about as an accident

when a scientist tried to create a brighter light bulb,
took semolina and poured it into the glass globe—

the effect reminded him of snowfall. But,
artificial snow, being enchanted, is a company secret

and when children show up at the snow globe factory,
their eyes must be wide open, they must be mesmerized

as they start shaking the globes all at once—
and the snow, depending upon the phase of moon, falls

everywhere, everywhere, but never melts and never sticks.

Acknowledgments

"Cento From the Mummy Doctor" appeared in *Puerto del Sol*

"Theta" won the *Texas Medicine and Literature Contest*, 2016

"Tangerines" appeared in *Fourth River*

"From Motor City Mulch" appeared in *Alyss*

"Today's List of Denials" appeared in *Body Language* (BOA Anthology Series)

CPSIA information can be obtained
at www.ICGtesting.com
Printed in the USA
BVHW070040110122
625846BV00001B/64